The

PI

PROJE

BOOK

The PVC PROJECT BOOK

101 Uses for PVC Pipe in the Home, Garden, Farm, and Workshop

CHARLES A. SANDERS

BURFORD BOOKS

Printed in the United States of America.

10   9   8   7   6   5   4   3   2   1

Library of Congress Cataloging-in-Publication Data
Sanders, Charles A., 1954–
     The PVC project book : 101 uses for PVC pipe in the home,
  garden, farm and workshop / Charles A. Sanders.
          p.   cm.
     ISBN 1-58080-127-7 (pbk.)
     1. Plastics craft.   2. Pipe, Plastic.   3. Polyvinyl chloride.
  4. Gardening—Equipment and supplies.   5. Home economics—
  Equipment and supplies.   I. Title.

TT297.S24   2004
745.57'2—dc22
2004013239

Contents

INTRODUCTION

One of the most important innovations in modern plumbing has been the development of PVC, CPVC, and related plastic pipe. These materials have enabled the average homeowner or builder to become an expert in installing plumbing anywhere it is needed around the home. The versatility, durability, and simplicity of the pipes and the dozens of different types of fittings and couplings make just about any project a snap.

Development and History of PVC

The plastic material that we refer to simply as PVC is actually made from a chemical compound called polyvinyl chloride. In 1912, a German researcher, chemist Fritz Klatte, set up a reaction in his laboratory between acetylene and hydrochloric acid (HCl). This produced a substance called vinyl chloride, but at that time no one knew what to do with it. It was put on the shelf, where it polymerized over time—creating what was considered merely a useless rigid material. Other scientists examining the new substance could find no commercial use for it. Not really knowing what to do with the PVC he had just invented, Klatte described it to his bosses at Greisheim Electron, who had the material patented in Germany. They never figured out a use for PVC, either, and in 1925 their patent expired.

Later, in 1926, Dr. Waldo Semon, a researcher at the B. F. Goodrich Company in Akron, Ohio, was attempting to find an adhesive that would bond rubber to metal. He began experimenting with the discarded material by combining it with other chemicals and exposing it to heat. The result was plasticized polyvinyl chloride—which we now call PVC or vinyl—a flexible "gel" that had striking similarities to natural rubber. Semon and Goodrich patented the material in the United States. Throughout the late 1920s, Semon continued to experiment with this new material, but Goodrich had a difficult time marketing it.

During the 1930s, vinyl (PVC or polyvinyl chloride) saw its first commercial application in the form of shock absorber seals. This initial use opened the eyes of industry to other possible applications that could help reduce the country's dependence on the world's limited rubber resources. Later, flexible vinyl was used to develop the first American synthetic tires, which we still run on our cars today. Those successes early on led to more experimentation with vinyl formulations.

It wasn't until the 1950s that vinyl began to reach the consumer market in a big way. Experimentation continued, and new variations were developed. Possibly the most important innovation came in 1952, when irrigation pipe made from rigid vinyl was introduced to the United States from Europe. Today, in what has become the largest market for vinyl production, PVC pipe is recognized as a less expensive, noncorrosive, and more easily installed alternative to metal pipe.

Like all PVC products, PVC pipe derives its properties from the specific combinations of additives and modifiers mixed with PVC resin. These include stabilizers, providing strength and durability; plasticizers, providing varying degrees of flexibility and resistance to ultraviolet (UV) light degradation; and pigments, used selectively to provide color. Once the additives and modifiers have been combined with the resin, the resulting material is called PVC compound, and is in granular form.

In the next stage of manufacturing, these granules are melted down, blended thoroughly, and extruded into pipe. The finished pipe is tested against nationally and internationally established standards, and guaranteed to be strong and safe through third-party certification.

Today, PVC is the predominant material used in drain, waste, and vent (DWV) applications. It is also used extensively in cold-water delivery systems to or for buildings.

PVC pipe is available in a variety of lengths, diameters, and pressure classes. It has a full complement of standard fittings, valves, and couplings. And it is compatible with other pipe materials, so it can be specified for either new construction or system upgrades.

PVC pipe is tough stuff. It is designed and manufactured to be that way. It provides time-tested resistance to costly leakage. It is corrosion resistant and reliable. PVC pipe is not a conductor of electricity, nor is it affected by excessively hard or soft water, changes in water pH, or the chemical constituents found in both domestic and industrial wastewater. When used in household plumbing systems, PVC pipe resists attack by cleaners and other household chemicals. Because PVC withstands conditions that other pipe materials cannot, it is frequently selected in place of, or to replace, other pipe materials.

PVC pipe is even flexible. It can bend without breaking. Both pipe and joint assemblies withstand pressure surges and shock. PVC pipe is resistant to impact, general wear, and abrasion, providing reliable service and less costly maintenance than other piping materials. With all this said, one of the best qualities of PVC pipe is simply that it is easy to work with.

The Right Stuff

Just so you know, when people talk about "plastic pipe" or "PVC pipe," they may actually be discussing any one of several types of plastic plumbing pipe. Let's take a look at some of the common ones:

- **ABS** or acrylonitrile-butadiene-styrene is a rigid plastic used for drain, waste, and vent piping in mobile homes as well as in residential and commercial sanitary systems. The pipe is black in color, crush resistant, and has an air temperature range of -40 to 180 degrees Fahrenheit. It comes in sizes from 1½ to 4 inches in diameter. ABS is strong, but light and easy to cut. ABS is joined with solvent glue and plastic fittings. Transition fittings are available to make connections to steel, copper, or cast iron. The use of ABS is restricted in some areas, so check your local codes first when using it.

- **PVC**, or polyvinyl chloride, is a synthetic material made from chlorine (derived from salt) and ethylene (composed of hydrogen and carbon and obtained from crude oil). Reactions between chlorine and ethylene create chloride monomer or VCM, and polymerization of VCM produces long chains or PVC. It is used for cold-water applications only. It is a white, rigid plastic and comes in 10- and 20-foot lengths. Schedule 40 is the most common choice for residential work; pipe from ½ inch to 2 inches in diameter is used for pressure applications, while pipe diameters of 1½ inches and up are used for drains, waste, and venting. Customary pressure applications include irrigation systems and the main water lines between the street and a residence. Schedule 300, 200, and 125 may also be used for irrigation systems. If you are using PVC for a supply line, be sure to choose pipe that has been approved for drinking by the National Sanitation Foundation (NSF). PVC is highly resistant to damage from heat or chemicals; it is joined with solvent glue and plastic fittings.

- **PVC tubing** is used to transport water. It is frequently used in fish tanks, fountains, pools, and spas.

- **CPVC** (chlorine-polyvinyl-chloride) is used mainly for hot-water applications in the home. The pipe is durable and fairly inexpensive. It commonly replaces copper pipe in interior applications. CPVC has a hard surface and requires a two-step joining procedure. First a primer is used to break down the hard surface; then solvent cement is used to join the pipe and fitting. CPVC pipe and fittings are pressure rated for continuous use at 400 pounds per square inch (psi) at 73.4 degrees Fahrenheit, and 100 psi at 180 degrees. As temperature increases, pressure rating decreases. Under no circumstances should temperatures exceed 212 degrees. Plastics are affected by ultraviolet radiation. Pigments are added to the CPVC to make pipe and fittings resistant to degradation. CPVC can be exposed to sunlight during construction, but prolonged exposure to the sun is not advised unless protected by a water-based latex paint.

- **PEX** (Cross-Linked Polyethylene) is used as both hot and cold interior water pipe in residential applications. PEX's flexibility makes it easy to maneuver around obstructions without using elbows. It ranges in size from ¼ to ¾ inch. PEX is joined with plastic grip or metal crimp fittings.

- **Funny Pipe** is used to put sprinkler heads in difficult spots. Made of high-strength poly tubing that acts like a flexible extension cord, it allows you to put sprinklers exactly where you want them. Funny Pipe can be installed under walkways or extended into hard-to-reach areas. It also helps you avoid having to retrench or change existing water lines. Funny Pipe comes in 100-foot rolls and is easy to cut.

- **Corrugated drainpipe** is black plastic pipe used primarily for drainage. It is available in 10-, 20-, or 100-foot lengths and in 3- to 15-inch diameters. The 3- and 4-inch pipe is used to carry water away from gutters or the foundation of a house. The 12- to 18-inch pipe is used as culvert drainage pipe for driveways and parking lots. The smaller-diameter pipe is available in perforated or slotted form. It is manufactured with small slots at close intervals and is buried in trenches to drain wet areas of lawns, pastures, fields, and so on.

PVC is used to make much more than pipe. Today, just about every new home is being sided in "vinyl" siding made from PVC. Vinyl floor coverings are also made from PVC. Everything from vinyl car tops to raincoats can be made from this useful compound.

As you can see, there are a variety of pipe materials designed for different applications. Not surprisingly, it wasn't long after the development of these revolutionary materials that the home craftsman was at work devising new and ingenious uses for them. There are myriad applications for PVC pipe and its cousins around the home, farm, garden, and workshop besides plumbing.

We will be dealing here, primarily, with Schedule 40 PVC pipe. All the projects described will call for that, unless otherwise noted.

Grades of PVC Pipe

PVC pipe identified as Schedule 40 DWV pipe, or informally as Schedule 40 pipe, is used for both above-grade and below-grade installations. Special 3¼-inch outside-diameter pipe, which has a thinner wall than Schedule 40 DWV, is referred to informally as Schedule 30 pipe. This pipe is made specifically to fit within a regular 2 × 4-inch-wide stud wall assembly.

PVC pipe does have its limitations. Plastics are affected by ultraviolet radiation. Pigments are added to the PVC to make pipe and fittings resistant to degradation. When used for domestic and general building applications, PVC can be exposed to sunlight during construction, but prolonged exposure to the sun is not advised. For most of our applications, the degree of photodegradation will be so slight that it will not be a concern. PVC pipe and fittings can withstand normal temperatures encountered in a sanitary and storm drainage system. The recommended maximum temperature for continuous drainage applications is 140 degrees Fahrenheit.

PVC pipe and fittings are pressure rated at 73.4 degrees. These ratings decrease as temperature increases.

PVC PLASTIC FURNITURE PIPE

Some PVC pipe is also available that is compounded and blended expressly for pipe furniture. It is made with the additions of titanium dioxide, weather inhibitors, and impact modifiers. The color will not fade, and it is extremely resistant against breakage. In minutes, you can make your own worktables, racks, and furniture with ordinary PVC plastic pipe. Simply cut measured lengths of the white plastic pipe with a hacksaw, slip on plastic fittings, and glue them in place.

Companies such as Genova and Lasco make fittings designed specifically for PVC furniture. These are available at most of the larger hardware outlets. Many smaller hardware stores simply don't have the demand to warrant stocking them. But diligent searching will help you find the ones you need. See the sources listed in the last chapter of this book for more information.

BLACK POLYETHYLENE ROLL PIPE

This pipe is strong, with a long life expectancy. It is excellent for water systems, drainage, and many other applications. It is not UV resistant since it is usually buried underground. A variety of fittings, reducers, couplers, and adapters are available. Fittings are made from either plastic or galvanized metal. The pipe is usually sold in 100-foot rolls in diameters from ½ inch to 1½ inches.

Working with PVC Pipe

BENDING AND SHAPING

Some of the projects in this book require PVC pipe to be bent. Although PVC pipe can be bent somewhat, more drastic shaping calls for other methods. To bend or shape PVC pipe, it must be temporarily softened. This is best done by heating it to the point where it is malleable, which can be accomplished in a number of ways:

• **Hot water**. Dip the piece to be worked into very hot or boiling water. Allow the pipe to heat completely through. As you work the piece, repeated dunkings into the hot water may be necessary.

- **Heat lamps**. An ordinary heat lamp can heat PVC pipe to workable temperatures. Allow it to get thoroughly heated, and resoften as needed.

- **Heaters**. I have heated pieces of PVC pipe over the burner of the kerosene heater that I use in my workshop. It quickly softened the ends of the pieces I was working. Again, reapply heat as the piece cools and hardens.

Once you have the piece softened sufficiently, you can bend it, pinch it, and shape it.

CUTTING AND SHAPING

PVC pipe should be cut square with a wheeled tubing cutter or fine-toothed saw such as a hacksaw. A handy cutter that resembles hand pruners is also available. The ratcheting action makes it simple to cut pipe up to 1 inch in diameter. In my experience, however, it is difficult to make a precisely square cut when using these cutters. If that is important for your project, then use a saw. Otherwise, the ratcheting cutters are great for general cutting of PVC pipe.

You can create a bell shape in the end of a piece of PVC pipe by heating it to a workable temperature and then shoving the end down over the top of a glass bottle—a wine bottle works well.

Before gluing, pipe ends should be de-burred and wiped clean and dry, free of any oil or dirt.

GLUING PVC PIPE

Use of special primer is recommended when gluing pipe, couplings, and fittings, especially when the pipes will be under pressure. Primer is a mixture of solvents used to penetrate the pipe and fittings and start the swelling process ahead of the application of the solvent cement. The primer is made not only to clean the surface of the pipe, but also to slightly soften the hard exterior and allow the glue to make a better bond.

Be sure that the pipe you are working with is dry. All solvent cements have the ability to absorb some water and still perform well enough to create an adequate joint. However, research shows that the presence of just 10 percent water in solvent cement can slow penetration and swelling by up to 65 percent. The affected joint, with water inside, will always be an inferior joint and subject to failure. There are many plastics that cannot be glued at all; these include polyethylene, polypropylene, nylon, polybutylene, and other polyolefins.

PAINTING PVC PIPE

As with any painting project, your goal is to apply a finish that is durable and wear resistant.

Prior to attempting to paint PVC, you must first give it a thorough cleaning to remove any grease, oil, or other contaminants that may be on its surface. After the surface is clean, use some fine sandpaper or fine steel wool to rough the finish just enough to help the coating adhere better. Since PVC is not really designed to be painted, apply the selected coating in a small test area and check to make sure it adheres well before continuing with the entire project.

You may use a coat of primer paint to help your final finish coat adhere better. I have successfully painted many PVC items, and as with anything else, I find that if the item is used frequently or roughly, some touch-up may be needed at some point. In some cases, such as painting a greenhouse frame, the surface preparation can generally be bypassed altogether, since the greenhouse frame is not going to be tossed around or receiving rough treatment.

Tools for PVC Pipe Projects

As you begin to use the ideas presented in this book, as well as coming up with many of your own, you will need a few basic tools on hand. Here's a list of the common ones needed for most of the projects discussed here:

• PVC pipe—various lengths and diameters

• PVC fittings—various assorted

• Pipe cutter

• Hacksaw

• Tape measure

• Pencils

• Pocketknife

• Sandpaper

• File

• PVC cleaner

• PVC glue

• Drill

• Screws

• Propane torch, heat bulb, or other device to heat pipe for bending or shaping

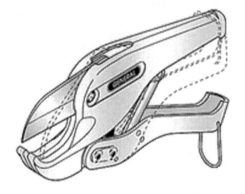

Ratcheting cutters are useful for making square cuts on PVC pipe.

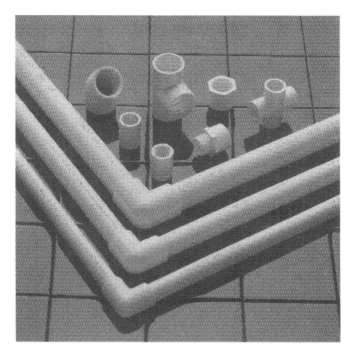

PVC pipe is versatile and easy to work with. COURTESY GENOVA PRODUCTS.

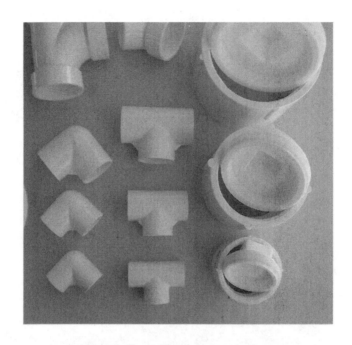

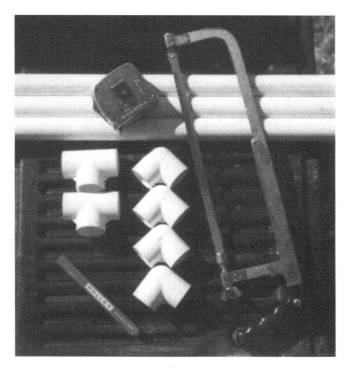

PVC projects call for common tools.

As you know by now, a wide variety of pipe, fittings, and couplings are available today. Most big hardware outlets and home supply stores will have what you need to work with PVC pipe. You might also want to check out some of the following Web sites, which offer pipe, materials, and specialized fittings for just about any project that you can come up with.

One note: Whenever working with PVC pipe, for whatever purpose, I recommend dry-fitting the pieces together before gluing them. This will allow you to check for final fit and placement of pipe and fittings. It's much easier to make a correction *before* you glue the pieces together than afterward.

SOURCES
- http://www.plumbingsupply.com/pvc.html
- http://www.littlegreenhouse.com/accessory/pvc.shtml
- http://www.greenhillmfg.com/pvccon.htm
- http://www.yardsupply.com/star/prodpages/pvc.htm
- http://www.usplastic.com/catalog/
- http://www.lascofittings.com
- http://www.genovaproducts.com

IN THE HOME

PVC Storage Container

Occasionally, you may be presented with the need to store, cache, or hide items. Perhaps you wish to hide your egg money in something other than a fruit jar. You may feel the need to put away a firearm and supply of ammunition. Or you may just have something of value that you would like to hide securely away from prying eyes. A simple and durable storage container can be made in a few minutes by using scraps of appropriately sized PVC pipe. All it takes is a section of pipe of the proper diameter and length for the item or items you wish to store. You can make these in 4-, 6-, 8-, 10-, or even 12-inch diameter.

Glue into place an end cap on one end of the pipe. On the other end, glue into place a collar with female threads to accept the same-sized male screw-in plug. You are all set.

When using your storage container, a desiccant may help prevent damage to the stored item. This is a simple and cheap process:

Merely toss into the container an old sock or other cloth bag filled with rice. The rice will serve as a very suitable moisture absorber. Or you can apply a bead of silicone sealer when you thread the cap into place. This will serve as a final moisture barrier.

Here's another tip. If you choose to put your container under-ground—that is, to bury it vertically in a posthole-type hole—then get a piece of black corrugated plastic drain tile in the next size larger than the PVC container you have. Dig the hole large enough to accommodate the black drain tile. Once it is in place, just drop in your PVC container. Cover with a large flat stone and cover with soil. If you are concerned about finding your storage site later, lay a piece of metal atop the stone before you cover it with earth. This will enable you to locate the site using a metal detector.

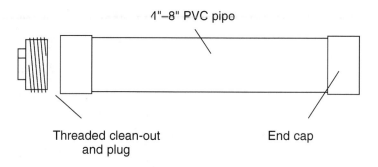

1"–8" PVC pipo

Threaded clean-out   End cap
and plug

A handy storage container can be made from any size of PVC pipe
and the appropriately sized fittings.

PVC Curtain Rod

It is not difficult to make a sturdy curtain rod from ordinary PVC pipe. Select the size that will fit through the end of your curtain or valance. Cut it to length and glue an elbow onto each end. Now mount two ordinary metal angle braces to the wall. Drill a couple of small holes in each elbow to match the holes in the braces, and mount the rod to the braces using small, tightly fitting machine screws.

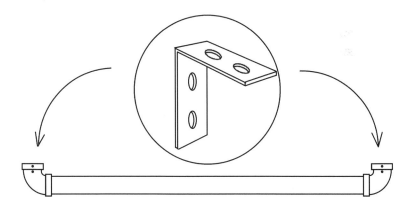

Make the curtain rod from 1½ or 2 inch
PVC pipe. Secure it to the wall by using
ordinary metal angle braces.

Even a curtain rod can be made from PVC pipe.

Clothes Rod/Rack

This clothes rack is made from some scraps of pipe and a few fittings. It is ideal for a college student or to put in the garage or wherever hunting clothes are stored.

You will need 1½-inch material for this project, including six elbows and four T's. Cut the top and bottom pieces about 32 to 36 inches long. If you make it too wide, the rod might sag with the weight of clothes on it.

The height of the rack is also a matter of choice; about chin high is handy for most folks. The base of the rack should be wide enough to prevent it from tipping over easily. If you cut each of the four leg pieces about 12 inches long, that should work nicely.

Cut the pieces of pipe to the size you want, and dry-fit everything together before gluing.

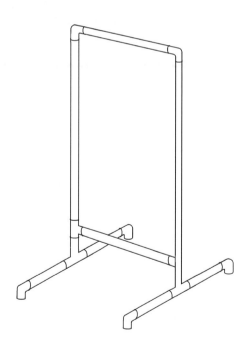

PVC scraps can be fashioned into a clothes rack.

Newspaper Box

If you need to attach a box to your mailbox post for your local newspaper, you can make one quickly with a piece of 4-inch PVC pipe and an end cap. Cut the pipe to a length that will accept the paper, and glue on the end cap.

You can attach the box to the post in a number of ways, depending on what you are working with. If you have a wooden post, you may want to use screws. If the post is a common 4 × 4 model, drill two holes in the paper box about 2½ inches apart along the length of the pipe. It will take a bit of time, but—using two appropriately sized hex-head lag screws and a ratchet—attach the box to the post.

You can also use heavy cable ties to attach the paper box. Put two around the box as far apart as the post is wide. Run one more cable tie through each of the first two, around the post, and secure. Tighten up all three snugly, and the box should be secure.

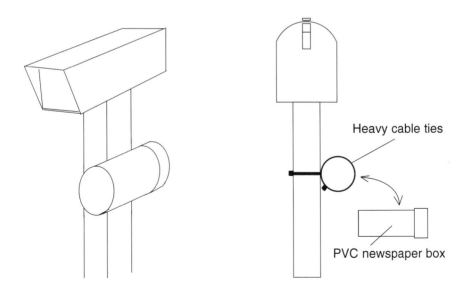

Heavy cable ties

PVC newspaper box

The PVC newspaper box.

Firewood Rack

A handy rack for holding firewood can be made from 2- or 3-inch PVC pipe. Granted, it won't hold a month's worth of wood, but it will hold a surprisingly large amount of fuel for your fireplace or stove.

Using four elbows and eight T's, along with some lengths of PVC pipe, you can turn out this firewood rack in an hour or less. Specific lengths for the pipes are not given here—your needs may vary. But on the average, if you make your rack about 3 feet long and 2 feet tall, sagging should not be a problem. If you want to make it longer, or just want to add some stability, check out the additional illustration that includes a set of support legs in the middle of the bottom pipes. This will help take care of any sagging that the weight of the wood might cause.

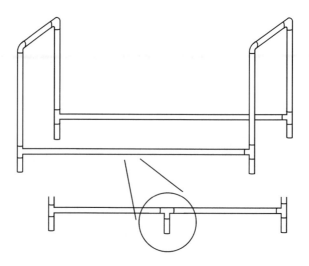

A firewood rack made from PVC pipe.

Soap Mold

If you enjoy making soap at home, try using pieces of 1½-, 2-, or 3-inch pipe cut into short lengths as a simple soap mold. Using duct tape, close one end of the mold by covering it with a piece of heavy plastic film. Two thicknesses are better. Pour in the soap "batter" and allow it to set up. Placing the soap-filled mold in the freezer should cause enough contraction that you can tap and shake the finished soap from the pipe mold. If it is still too snug to remove, try heating it a bit with a hair dryer. It should slip out easily.

Gutter Cleaner 1

If you need a good way to flush out your gutters without doing a balancing act on the extension ladder, try this trick. Use a female-threaded PVC coupler for attaching to a garden or washing machine hose. Glue it to an appropriate length of ¾-inch PVC pipe. Add a 90-degree elbow, a length of PVC pipe about 6 to 8 inches long, and a 45-degree elbow. To that, add a 3- to 4-inch piece of pipe. Attach the wand to a shutoff coupler on the hose end—and you're in business.

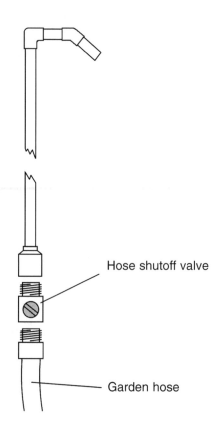

Hose shutoff valve

Garden hose

Use PVC to clean your gutters.

Gutter Cleaner 2

Here is another gutter cleaner that you might like to try. This one uses air instead of water.

Select a piece of PVC pipe that will fit over the end of your leaf blower pipe. This may require splitting the PVC pipe and shoving it over the end of the leaf blower. Make it a length convenient to reach your gutters. Add a couple of 45-degree elbows with a short piece on the end and you should be able to blow dried leaves and debris right out of your gutters using the power of the leaf blower.

Mailbox Post

A good PVC mailbox post can be made similarly to the post for a birdhouse or feeder (see the next chapter). You will need a section of 4-inch PVC pipe and a PVC stool flange.

Cut the pipe to the length you will need, including the portion that will be set in the ground. Glue the flange to the top of the post. Cut a board to fit the bottom of the mailbox and screw it to the stool flange. Attach the mailbox and set the post by digging a hole 2½ to 3 feet deep. It is a good idea to drill a couple of holes on opposite sides of the pipe and run a rod or pipe through before setting the post. This will keep the post from turning in the hole.

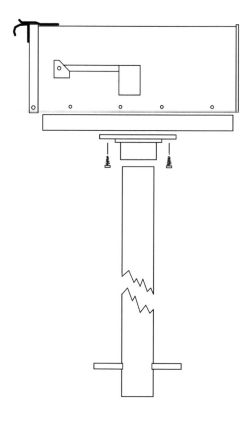

The mailbox post calls for PVC pipe and a stool flange.

2

IN THE GARDEN

Row Hoops

Possibly one of the best uses for joints of ½-inch PVC pipe is to create a miniature greenhouse in your garden. Combined with a sheet of heavy, clear plastic, this pipe can make a great growing-season extender in your own garden no matter how large a plot you have.

To construct your row covers, you will first need to cut twice as many 18-inch pieces of ¼-inch reinforcement rod (commonly called rebar) as you have pieces of PVC pipe. Here on our place, I simply used light metal electric-fence posts. They worked very well.

Drive in one rebar or fence post where you want the end of the PVC pipe to be. Continue down along either side of the row at about 3- or 4-foot intervals. Directly across the row or seedbed, set another post. Place one end of the ½-inch pipe over one of the posts. Bend the pipe over like a hoop on an old covered wagon and slide it down over the other post. Repeat this down the row until you have set out the number of hoops you need.

Cut the plastic plenty long, so that you can gather it up and anchor it at the ends with a big rock or block. Allow for an extra 12 to 18 inches on either side as well. I used this extra plastic to help anchor the little structure. Simply take a piece of pipe or conduit, and, with a helper, hold the edge of the plastic to the pipe and roll it up over the pipe. After rolling it up a few times around the pipe, lay a block or rock on either end of the pipe to anchor the plastic.

Row hoops at work in the early garden.

PVC Birdhouse

Excellent birdhouses can be made from scrap pieces of 4-inch pipe. For example, to make fine bluebird houses, take a section of 4-inch pipe about 9 inches long. To one end, glue an end cap. Just below the end cap on the main tube, use a door lockset hole drill and bore the 1¼-inch hole that is ideal for bluebirds. About ½ inch from the bottom of the tube's open end, drill two holes about ⅛ inch diameter and about 1½ inches apart. Directly across the diameter of the tube, repeat the procedure. You may make two or three shallow cuts with a saw directly below the entrance hole. This will permit the adult birds approaching the box to get a grip on it as they prepare to enter. Cut one of these deep enough that it makes a slot completely through the pipe about an inch long. This will be used for the next step.

Cut a piece of ¼- or ½-inch hardware cloth about the same diameter as the pipe. Insert it flatly into the bottom of the tube. This will be the actual bottom of the birdhouse. Through the four ⅛-inch holes that you drilled near the bottom of the tube, insert a U-shaped piece of wire and bend the ends to secure it. This will hold the hardware cloth floor in place.

Here is a variation on the PVC birdhouse. Make them with the materials you have.

You may wish to use a different type of bottom in the birdhouse. This can be done by slipping another end cap onto the bottom of the birdhouse in place of the wires and hardware cloth. Once the cap is in place, drill two pilot holes and secure it with a couple of self-tapping screws ½ to ¾ inch long. This will enable you to remove the bottom of the box seasonally for cleaning.

Another simple bluebird house made from PVC pipe.

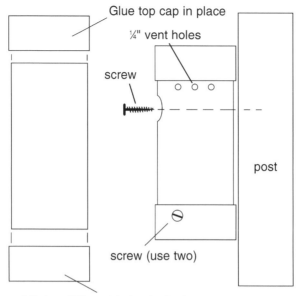

Glue top cap in place

¼" vent holes

screw

post

screw (use two)

drill 4 or 5 ¼" vent holes in the bottom

Yet another simple birdhouse made from PVC.

The birdhouse in place. Note the row hoops in the background.

PVC Hanging Planter

An attractive hanging planter can be made from PVC pipe. To create your planter, first locate a piece of 4-inch PVC pipe in the length you would like for your planter; something in the area of 16 to 24 inches works well.

Next, bore 1½-inch-diameter holes in the pipe at points where you want plants. I spaced the holes in staggered rows up and down the pipe; a row of three, turn the pipe 90 degrees, then a row of two. Add another row of three and another row of two, turning the pipe as you go.

Next, glue an end cap onto the bottom of the pipe with regular PVC cement. Near the center of the end cap, drill three or four small holes to allow for water drainage. At the top of the pipe, drill three holes about ⅛ inch in diameter at points dividing the circumference of the pipe into thirds.

To hang the planter, you can use twine, wire, chain—whatever you have handy. I used four small S-hooks and some light chain. Equal lengths of chain (about 12 to 14 inches) were attached to the three small holes using

The hanging planter.

S-hooks. The three pieces of chain were joined at the top by the fourth hook.

You can now add soil and your plants. You may also add a watering tube to the planter if you wish. Merely take a piece of ¾-inch PVC pipe about ½ to 1 inch longer than the planter and drill several small holes up and down its length. Position the small pipe in the center of the planter as you fill it with soil. You will end up with soil packed around the hollow center tube that will permit water to evenly reach all the plants.

This planter works especially well with plants such as geraniums, or other compact bushy flowers. Compact strawberries could also be planted in one of these.

Carryall Handle

I used an old wooden grape crate and made a handy carrier for garden plants. I used small wire staples to attach some stiff wire to both sides of one end of the crate. I ran the wire through a piece of ½-inch PVC pipe and out the other end before securing the wires to the opposite end of the crate. The result was a good, sturdy carrying handle for the crate.

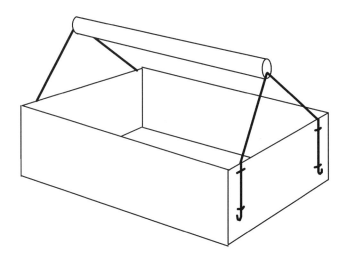

*This handy garden carryall has a simple
PVC pipe handle for rigidity.*

Tomato Stakes

Leftover lengths of PVC pipe make excellent tomato stakes. I like to cut the ends at an angle using my band saw. Make them from ½-inch pipe when you are anchoring wire tomato cages, or use 1- to 1½-inch pipe when using them alone to stake the plants.

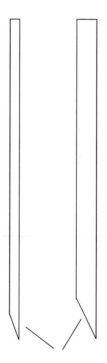

Cut the ends at an angle to make
them easy to drive into the soil

Tomato stakes can be easily made from scraps of PVC pipe.

Tomato Cages

Tomato cages can be made from PVC pipe. All it takes is some scrap ½- or ¾-inch pipe and some T's. In the illustration, you can see one half of the tomato tower. Each of the two crosspieces should be about 12 to 18 inches long. That will give plenty of growing room and support to the plants. Dry-fit each half together before gluing. Join the halves with more crosspieces. Glue them into towers and place them over your plants before they get too large. You can also make them taller by simply adding more sections above the top T.

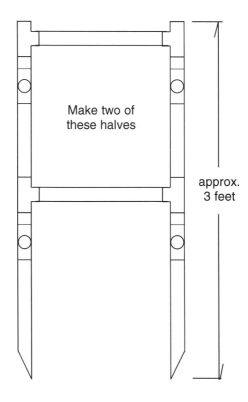

Half of the PVC tomato tower is visible here.

Cold Frame Cover

I made this cover for my cold frame from 1-inch PVC pipe and a few fittings. It was designed and cut to fit the area that I had to cover. I cut the pieces to fit and then put it all together without glue to make sure everything fit properly. Next, the whole thing was glued together. I added some strong greenhouse plastic by doubling the ends and attaching it with screws and washers, making sure it was pulled taut all across the frame. Then I simply put it in place to protect the small plants in my cold frame.

This cold frame cover was dry-fitted before gluing.

The cover with plastic in place.

DIY Sprinkler for Greenhouse and Garden

Ever wish you had an extra arm to reach those plants up high or way back in the planting bed when watering? You can easily make a watering wand for your garden hose by using a female ¾-inch threaded-to-straight fitting, an angle fitting, an appropriate length of ¾-inch pipe, and a sprinkler head.

Most sprinkler-can heads will fit a standard garden-hose-type thread, which is exactly what a male ¾-inch PVC fitting is. If you can pick up a replacement sprinkler head at your hardware store, it will screw right onto the end of your sprinkler wand. If not, try making one from a couple of PVC adapters and a 2-inch end cap. Using a fine drill bit, drill several holes in the end cap to allow the water to shower out.

Bird Feeder

A simple and easy bird feeder can be made from a short piece of 4-inch PVC pipe, an end cap, some stiff wire, and an old pie pan.

First, cut your pipe in the length that you want your feeder to be. Fourteen to 18 inches is good. Slide the end cap onto one end of the pipe. Just below where the cap fits, drill a couple of small holes that will take a piece of wire; you will later suspend the feeder from this.

On the other end, saw out a few notches around the circumference of the pipe. A couple of inches up from this end, drill two more small holes.

Drill two small holes in the bottom of the pie pan at points that will line up with the last two holes you drilled in the pipe, or close to it. Now run each end of a length of wire from the pan bottom up and through the small holes, from the inside out. Bend the ends of the wire down to securely hold the pan in place.

You can see in the illustration that the wire will hold the pan in place while the notches you cut in the bottom of the pipe will allow bird feed to settle into the pan. It is also a good idea to drill several small holes in the pie pan to allow rainwater to drain.

Cut a piece of wire to use as the hanger. Bends on each end of the wire are inserted into the holes near the top of the pipe. Now just remove the end cap to fill the feeder, then hang it in a good spot near some cover. The birds will soon find it.

You may also paint the feeder as you wish—a solid color, or add some hand-painted flowers, or what have you.

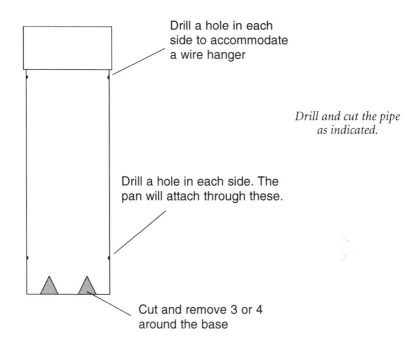

Drill a hole in each side to accommodate a wire hanger

Drill and cut the pipe as indicated.

Drill a hole in each side. The pan will attach through these.

Cut and remove 3 or 4 around the base

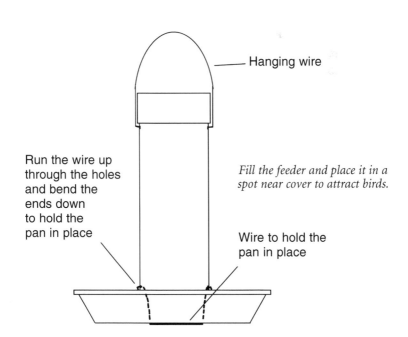

Hanging wire

Run the wire up through the holes and bend the ends down to hold the pan in place

Fill the feeder and place it in a spot near cover to attract birds.

Wire to hold the pan in place

Squirrel-Proof Bird Feeder Post

If you are erecting a birdhouse or feeder on a wooden post, squirrels and raccoons can become real pests. Try this to keep the furry pilferers from climbing up the post. Simply use a section of 4-inch PVC pipe as your post. Uninvited critters will not be able to climb the slick surface of the PVC pipe.

The addition of a toilet flange at the top of the post can provide a sturdy mount for your birdhouse or feeder.

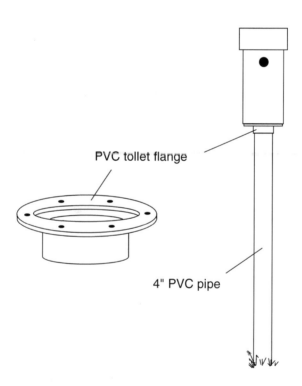

PVC toilet flange

4" PVC pipe

A PVC post and toilet flange makes a sturdy and pest-proof support for a birdhouse or feeder.

Seed Planter

If you are getting old enough that it really hurts to bend, then this handy seed planter might help. Just take a piece of ¾- or 1-inch PVC pipe about 32 to 36 inches long—a handy waist height. If you have a hard time getting the seeds in the pipe, use a few reducers to get the size of the upper end up to 2 or 3 inches. Then drop in the seeds; they will fall into place in the row as you move along. You can put the seeds right where you want them using this simple device.

If you use 1½-inch pipe, this handy device will also let you put your onion sets just where you want them without bending and stooping.

Pinwheel Holder

Attach a piece of ½-inch PVC pipe to a post or stake and drop in a toy pinwheel. The toy will spin freely in the slightest breeze and will be able to turn into the wind no matter which direction it is coming from. This will be a big help in keeping birds out of the blueberry or raspberry patch.

Hosta Ring

A simple hosta ring will help keep weeds down and permit up-close edging of these decorative plants with a weed trimmer. Using 8-inch PVC pipe, cut a section about 6 to 8 inches long. Either work this ring down over your existing plant or put it in place before you set out your hostas. This protective collar will help keep weeds from infesting your plants, and it can also make weed trimming easier by permitting a weed whacker to get up close without damaging the plant.

Orchard Limb Spreader

Occasionally, young fruit trees need some training to grow into the desired shape. Limb spreaders are commonly used to accomplish this. Some simple limb spreaders can be made from ¾-inch PVC pipe. First, cut some lengths of pipe that you think you'll need. Next, heat the ends of the pipe to the point that they are somewhat pliable. Tap the ends flat with a hammer or squeeze them in a bench vise. After the pipe cools, cut a shallow notch into each end of the pipe.

Limb spreaders fashioned from PVC pipe scraps.

Tool Holder 1

It seems that we are always misplacing our garden shears. My wife uses them frequently in and around her flower garden. To help keep them in a spot where we can find them, I made this simple holder from a scrap of 2-inch PVC pipe.

I bored a hole in one side large enough to insert a wood screw. Directly across the diameter of the pipe, I drilled a small hole to accommodate the screw, which is inserted into a wall stud in the tool shed. In just a couple of minutes, the shears are in their holder and ready to use next time.

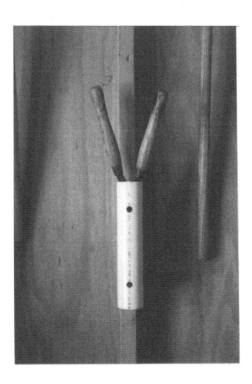

This holder for the garden shears keeps them protected and within easy reach.

Planter Hanger

This handy planter hanger can easily be made from a single piece of 4-inch PVC pipe, two elbows, and about 8 feet of light chain. That will give you plenty of pipe to put in the ground and also hang a flower box from. The measurements are not critical; just use what you have or can fit into the project, and make it whatever size suits you. Make a flower box from 1-inch-thick treated lumber in a size compatible with the PVC stand. Hang it from the long center pipe using the chain (wire or other material can be substituted).

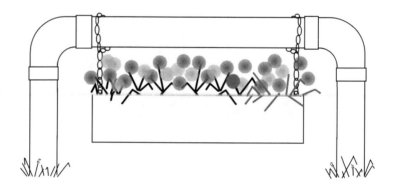

This attractive planter can be made easily and quickly.

Grape Arbor

A durable grape arbor can be easily made by using 4-inch PVC pipe and some fittings. You will need six 10-foot pieces of 4-inch pipe, four elbows, and four T's. Depending upon the width of your arbor, you may also need another 10-foot section or two of pipe.

To begin, I'd recommend dry-fitting all the pieces except the four uprights. This will make it easy to determine where to mark the spots to dig the postholes for the uprights.

If you want to make your arbor 5 feet wide by 10 feet long, then cut a 10-foot section in two. If you want the arbor to be a full 10 × 10 feet, then two pieces will be needed.

Assemble the pieces as shown in the diagram. Mark the locations for the holes. Dig the holes 2 to 2½ feet deep and set the posts. Assemble the pieces using PVC cement. Tamp the posts in firmly.

You can drill holes in the cross members and run wire from one side to the other to provide added support for the grapevines.

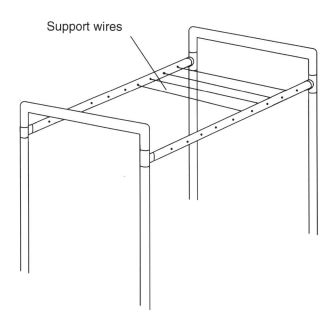

This grape arbor was made from 4-inch PVC pipe.

Garden Trellis

It isn't difficult to make a neat garden trellis from five pieces of ½-inch PVC pipe and a couple of pieces of treated lumber.

The bottom of the trellis is secured in a wooden block. This can be a piece of 2 × 4 cut about 12 inches long. I recommend using treated wood, because it will likely rest on the ground. Drill five blind holes about 1 inch deep and large enough to accommodate the pipe you are using. Space the holes evenly across the block. Insert the pipes into the holes, then drill a small hole through the wood and the pipe. Tap a nail into each hole and through the pipe to secure it in place.

Next, cut a strip of treated board to slide over the pipes and spread them apart. Use a piece of ordinary 1-inch lumber (actually about ⅝ inch thick) and about 24 inches long. Rip the board to 2 inches in width. Measure and mark five evenly spaced holes across the length of the board. These holes will need to be just a bit larger than the diameter of the pipe to allow for the angling out of the pipes as they are spread.

Slide the spacer down over pipes until you get the width you want in the spread pipes. Secure the spacer in place by drilling through it and into the pipe. Insert a small nail or screw.

A second spacer bar will provide rigidity to the trellis. Measure the spread on the pipes onto another wood strip and drill holes to accommodate. Slide it into place and secure it with nails as described.

Now all that is left is to anchor the trellis near your climbing plants and wait for your morning glories or other vining plants to make the climb.

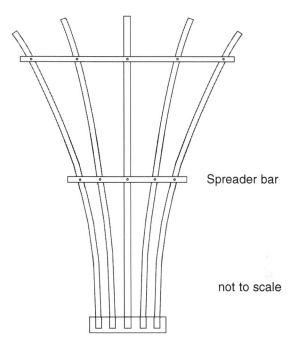

Spreader bar

not to scale

A garden trellis can be made easily from PVC pipe.

Bore holes 1 inch deep to
accommodate the ½" PVC pipe

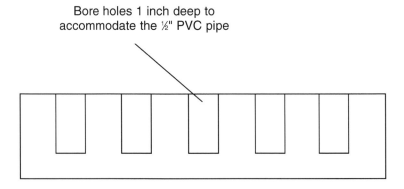

A wooden block is used to anchor the pipes for the garden trellis.

Garden Gate

A nifty arch for your garden entrance can be put together out of 1½-inch PVC pipe and some fittings. You will need 12 T's, two 90-degree elbows, four 45-degree elbows, and four joints of pipe. Study the illustration to see the location of each fitting. Make two of the halves shown, then join them with six crosspieces 18 to 32 inches long.

Make the arch to suit your needs as to width and height. It should be about 2 feet deep for stability. Set the legs in holes and fill with dirt or gravel. If you wish, plant some morning glories or other vining plants around the base and allow them to climb to the top.

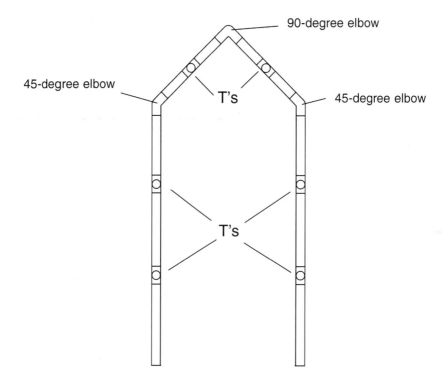

One half of the garden gate is shown. Make two and join them with pieces of pipe.

3

BUILDING
THE PVC
GREENHOUSE

The design and construction of a PVC greenhouse is involved enough to warrant a separate chapter on the topic.

There are as many designs for these versatile structures as there are people building them. Simply use what you have and make it to suit your needs. Below are a few ideas and variations for building your own PVC greenhouse.

Greenhouse Using a 2 x 6 Frame

PVC pipe can be valuable in erecting a simple, yet very functional and durable greenhouse.

On a good level spot, stake off the spot where your greenhouse is to be built. A good size for most home growers is 10 or 12 feet by 16 to 20 feet. This size range will give you plenty of room to start your plants, then get them separated out and growing. Be sure the site is squared so that your plastic will fit.

Create a base for the hoops by anchoring treated 2 × 6s on edge. They will sit right on top of the ground. Attach conduit clamps to the inside run of the 2 × 6s. These will be where you insert the ends of the PVC pipe. Conduit clamps are shaped, galvanized strips of metal formed to go over a piece of pipe or conduit. Holes for anchoring the clamps are predrilled. Your hardware store should carry them.

You will also probably need to drive 2-foot-long pieces of metal pipe at a few places along the length of the 2 × 6s, on the outside. This will prevent the PVC pipe from spreading the 2 × 6s apart. Drill a hole near the end of this pipe and attach it to the 2 × 6 with a ¼-inch lag screw. This will help anchor the structure to the ground during strong winds.

Use conduit clamps to hold the base in place, securing them to treated 2 × 6s. By locating the clamps on the inside of the 2 × 6 frame, you get the benefit of the boards holding the arched pipes more firmly in place. You can also anchor the plastic to the board frame. A few pieces of rebar or metal pipes driven along the outside of the 2 × 6s will help anchor them in place. If you have a low spot or two along the bottom of the frame, merely seal it up with a few shovelfuls of dirt.

Frame in the ends using whatever lumber you have on hand. You can cover the ends with plastic or plywood. I've seen both done. Be certain to allow for plenty of ventilation. Windows and vents are essential to keeping the temperature regulated. This, in turn, will help keep plants alive and prolong the life of your greenhouse covering. An old storm door makes a good entryway for the structure.

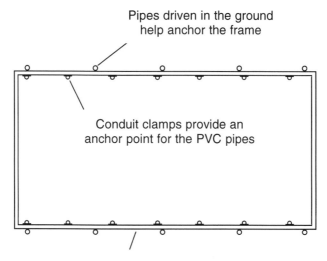

Pipes driven in the ground
help anchor the frame

Conduit clamps provide an
anchor point for the PVC pipes

Frame of treated 2 × 6's provides a solid base

Top view of the greenhouse frame.

Secure the end PVC hoops to your frame using clamps or carefully drilled holes and screws or nails. If you use these fasteners, cover the heads with a piece of duct tape to help prevent wearing a hole in the plastic where they protrude.

It's time to stretch the plastic. Make sure your covering is large enough to reach over the entire arch, with a foot or so to spare on either side. Also, be sure to allow some overlap on the ends to tuck and wrap.

Begin by attaching one edge of the plastic to the board frame. Do this by doubling the edge of the plastic over on itself to make two or three thicknesses. Hold it securely in place along the frame and cover the thicknesses with a wooden strip. Nail through the strip and the plastic and into the frame. Space the nails every 18 inches or so; closer doesn't hurt. I use aluminum roofing nails for this. They have a large head and do not rust.

Now stretch the plastic good and tight over the frame. You will need help for this chore, too. Two or three helpers is great. One is essential.

On the second side, with the plastic stretched tight, again fold
the plastic over itself or wrap it around a wooden lath strip. Nail it
securely in place just as you did on the first side.

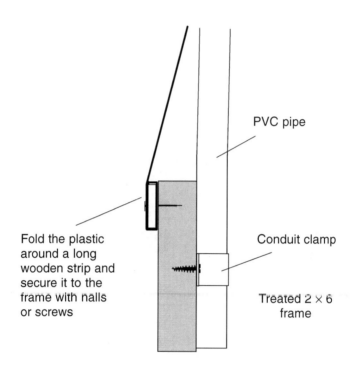

PVC pipe

Fold the plastic
around a long
wooden strip and
secure it to the
frame with nails
or screws

Conduit clamp

Treated 2 × 6
frame

With the plastic firmly in place, it's time to secure the ends. You
will need to fold and tuck the plastic as you work your way over the
arch and down the other side. Short strips of lath are useful here to
secure the covering into the wooden ends you have constructed.

As for the ends themselves, if they are not completely made of
wood, cover them as needed with pieces of plastic, held firmly with
nailed strips. Remember to allow for ventilation by providing windows, louvers, fans, and so forth. Keeping the temperature regulated
will greatly prolong the life of your structure.

When it comes to the plastic itself, note that ordinary roll plastic
that you buy at the hardware store will not work as a greenhouse

covering. Even if you are successful in getting the greenhouse covered with it, it will only last a few months before it begins to tear, shred, and fragment. Greenhouses call for special coverings. One of the best I have found is a durable woven plastic that has a solid layer bonded to each side of it. It is treated to resist UV degradation and is very durable. This material is available from Northern Greenhouse Sales, P.O. Box 42, Neche, ND 58265; 204-327-5540. I really like the products offered by Robert Davis at NGS.

Now all that is left is to get some benches or tables in the structure and put it to work growing all the plants you've dreamed of.

Greenhouse Using Railroad Ties

You can erect a greenhouse similar to the one above by using railroad ties instead of the 2 × 6s for the frame. Bore holes through the ties and anchor them with lengths of pipe or rebar. Bore larger holes to accommodate the bends of pipe that you will be inserting. Anchor the plastic to the ties themselves, using lath strips for added support. The ends of the structure can be framed in as described above.

Another Good Greenhouse Design

The accompanying photos illustrate a greenhouse that was built by some friends. They framed the sides of the structure with 2 × 4 short walls. The arched PVC pipes were anchored in 45-degree PVC couplings that were, in turn, attached to short lengths of pipe. Those short pieces were anchored to the 2 × 4 frame, providing a solid support to the arched roof. The ends were made of regular framing lumber and plywood. Conduit anchors were used throughout the structure for securing the pipe to the frame, and for securing the arches to the straight support pipes to provide even more rigidity. My friends told me one secret to the process: Paint the PVC pipe with white latex paint. It protects the pipe from ultraviolet degradation and greatly extends the life of the structure. I think this might be more important in a structure like this, whose pipes are bent into arches and under some stress.

Detail of anchoring the PVC pipe to the wooden frame.
Note the use of two conduit clamps per pipe.

Another detail showing the attachment of the PVC pipe to the wooden
frame. Note the use of two conduit clamps to anchor the pipe.

4

AROUND
THE FARM

PVC Electric-Fence Handle

Electric fences are versatile, easy to put up, and effective. Often, though, the homesteader may come upon a stretch of fence where a gate is needed. A cheap and easy version of an electric-fence gate handle can be made using scrap pieces of ¾- or 1-inch PVC pipe. Take a piece of pipe about 8 to 10 inches long and drill two small holes through one end. Use a long, sturdy coil spring—which will fit up inside the pipe—and secure it by using a slender bolt and nut through the holes. The open coil on the protruding end of the spring will serve to hook the loop of electric fence and secure the gate. Tailor the length of pipe to fit the spring you have available; just be sure to make it long enough that your hand does not come in contact with the fence wire or spring.

If you do not have a suitable spring, you can still make the gate handle. Merely run the electric-fence wire through the pipe and twist a small closed loop on the end. Drill two small holes through the pipe. Take a heavy piece of wire (number 9 or 12 wire is fine) and bend it into a hook. Run the heavy wire through one of the holes, through the fence wire loop, and out through the other hole in the pipe. Bend the hook wire to secure it in place.

Either of these simple handles will allow you to open and close a stretch of electric fence without turning it off or jumping clear out of your boots.

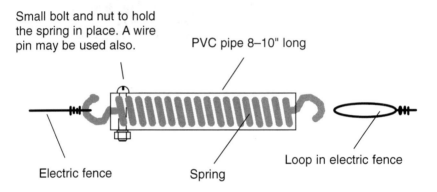

Small bolt and nut to hold the spring in place. A wire pin may be used also.

PVC pipe 8–10" long

Electric fence

Spring

Loop in electric fence

An electric-fence gate handle made from PVC and a spring.

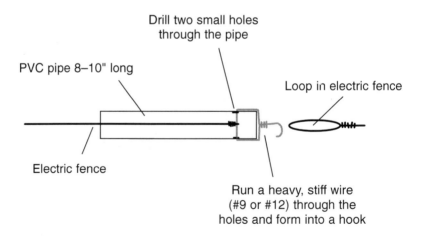

Drill two small holes through the pipe

PVC pipe 8–10" long

Loop in electric fence

Electric fence

Run a heavy, stiff wire (#9 or #12) through the holes and form into a hook

Another easy-to-make electric fence handle made from PVC pipe and a short piece of wire.

Wildlife, Livestock, or Pet Feeder

Using a piece of 4-inch PVC pipe approximately 4 feet long, glue a threaded clean-out on one end. On the other end, glue a Y. Now find a piece of pipe about 5 to 6 inches long, and glue it into the bottom end of the Y. To that, glue in place another threaded clean-out. This handy feeder can be tied or wired onto a post or tree and used to feed farm animals such as goats or sheep, or wildlife. Merely remove the top threaded cap, pour the pipe full of feed, and replace the cap. To occasionally clean out the feeder, you can simply remove the bottom clean-out plug, clean the feeder, replace the plug, and refill.

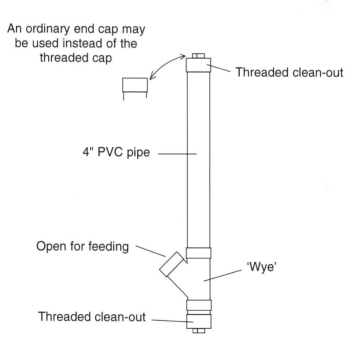

This simple feeder can be used for all sorts of animals.

Drip for Dust Control

If you live on a gravel road, you know how dusty it can get during the dry summer months. You can make a device to attach to a truck-mounted water tank that will help ease your dusty coughing.

First, determine the size of valve that you have coming out of your water tank (2½ to 3 inches is common). You will need to purchase a female-to-straight PVC coupler in that size. Glue a piece of straight pipe into the coupler, then attach to it one end of a rubber soil stack coupler using the hose clamp provided. Thread the assembly onto the tank valve.

For the water distributor, first take a T and glue a 6-inch piece of pipe into it as shown in the illustration. Into the legs of the T, glue in long pieces of pipe that will reach either side of your truck or so (3 to 4 feet should be plenty). Attach end caps to the ends of these two pieces. Along the length of these pipes, drill ⅛-inch holes spaced a couple of inches apart.

Attach the distributor to the tank by inserting the short pipe into the rubber coupler. Position the distributor on or just over the back of the truck bed. Tighten the clamp firmly. The rubber coupler should provide enough give to prevent stress breaks in the PVC pipe as the truck bumps along.

All that is left is to fill the water tank, crack the valve, and drive along in front of your house, letting the water settle the dust. In some areas, you can used approved oils (such as soy oil) instead of water.

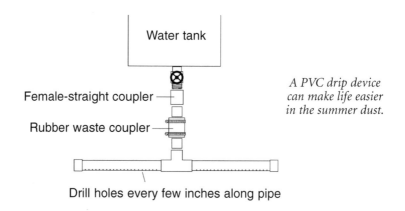

Water tank

Female-straight coupler —

Rubber waste coupler —

A PVC drip device can make life easier in the summer dust.

Drill holes every few inches along pipe

Riser for a Buried Water Valve

Starting with a piece of 8-inch-diameter PVC pipe, cut it about 2–3 feet longer than the valve is buried. Next, cut two slots a bit greater than the diameter of the water line itself and about 6 to 8 inches deep. Before you backfill the hole around the water-line valve, place the 8-inch riser pipe down over the water line, with the slots over the line. Work it firmly into the soil, then backfill the rest of the hole. The riser will keep the buried valve accessible. In areas of heavy freezing, you can fill the pipe with pieces of Styrofoam or insulation bats, then cover with a PVC cap if necessary to help keep the valve and line from freezing.

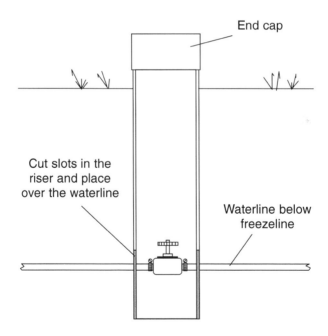

End cap

Cut slots in the
riser and place
over the waterline

Waterline below
freezeline

A PVC riser will keep your water valve from freezing.

Sprayer Holder

A sawed-off piece of 10-inch PVC pipe is bolted or wired onto the corner of the front box to hold a hand pump sprayer containing weed spray.

You can glue an end cap onto the pipe and, using two U-bolts, attach it to the cargo rack of your ATV.

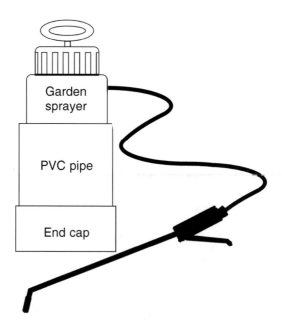

A PVC holder makes weed spraying easier.

Hand Pump Pipe

We have an old hand pump sitting atop an old hand-dug well that we have used to water our cattle. When I installed the pump, I used 1½-inch PVC pipe. On the bottom end of the pipe, I attached an ordinary foot valve. This valve prevents water from draining out of the pipe and makes pumping water much easier, since you do not have to prime the pump every time you use it. This is a great setup for warm weather or in areas that do not experience freezing weather.

Here in southern Indiana, however, we regularly get winter temperatures of 0 degrees Fahrenheit, and sometimes as low as -20 to -30 degrees. Temperatures that cold can make quick work of cast-iron pumps and plastic pipe. Preventing this is easily done, however. Pull the pump and pipe up out of the well. Drill a small hole in the PVC pipe at a point above below the normal winter water level. For normal summer operation of the pump, merely fill the hole with a snugly fitting self-tapping screw. That will allow the water to remain in the pipe and eliminate the need for priming the pump each time it is used. Come winter, you'll need to raise the pump and pipe and remove the screw. That will allow the water to drain out of the pipe as far as the hole and eliminate the chance of the pipe and pump freezing and bursting. You will need to either keep a bucket

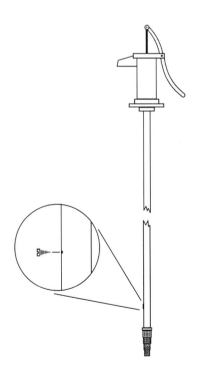

PVC pipe can keep a hand pump operational all year.

of water at the well to use in priming the pump, or carry one with you from the house to the well.

Be sure, when drilling the hole, not to make it too large, or the pump will suck air, making it difficult to draw water. Try a short number 6 or 7 self-tapping screw and appropriately sized hole.

This simple alteration should help you keep your hand pump operational year-round.

Banner Frame

To advertise your farm market, your produce stand, or even a yard sale, you need a sign. This PVC banner frame can help.

Depending upon the size of the sign or banner you plan to use, follow these general directions. Take one piece of 1½- to 4-inch PVC pipe a bit longer than the length of the sign you will be posting. Attach elbows to each end of the pipe. To an identical piece of pipe, attach two T's. Connect the two long pieces with two pieces just a bit longer than the height of your sign. Add lengths of pipe to the open end of the T's to put into the ground or over stakes to elevate the sign. The finished frame will resemble an old bed headboard.

This banner frame is made from a few fittings and some scraps of PVC pipe.

A frame made from 4-inch PVC pipe holds a sign advertising real estate.

Chain Saw Guard

I keep a piece of 4-inch PVC pipe over the bar of my chain saw to protect the sharp chain. I hold it in place with a bungee cord. When hauling the saw on my ATV or in my truck, the bar and chain are covered and protected.

This simple guard protects the chain saw chain.

Feed Trough

This simple feeder can be made from a scrap piece of large-diameter PVC pipe. Four-inch will work, but 6- or 8-inch diameter is better. It is ideal for goats and sheep and will work for calves if made from the larger-diameter pipe.

Simply cut the pipe in half lengthwise. Add ends by using one of these two methods:

1. Using the pipe end as a template, trace the half-moon shape onto a piece of 1-inch lumber. Cut out two of the pieces and attach to the ends of the pipe by drilling through the pipe in several places and nailing it in place.

2. Or you can slip an ordinary PVC end cap in place on the half and mark it where the sides of the trough end. Carefully cut the end cap in two; glue the halves on either end of the trough.

This rugged feeder can be mounted on a barn wall, between studs, or in any dry, sturdy place.

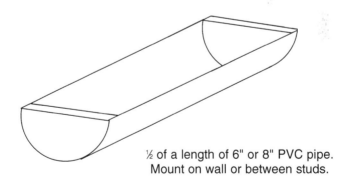

½ of a length of 6" or 8" PVC pipe.
Mount on wall or between studs.

The PVC feed trough.

Hanging Feed Trough

This is a variation on the feeder described above. When making the end pieces of wood, use a scrap of 2 × 6. The additional thickness will provide a place to insert a heavy screw eye. From the screw eyes, suspend the trough from a rafter or other overhead point. Hanging the trough in the center of the feed area allows animals to access it from all sides.

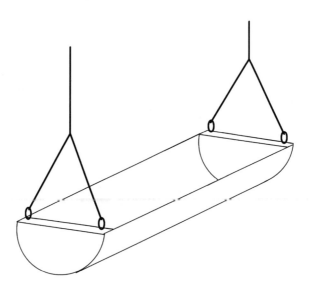

A hanging feed trough.

Chicken-Proof Chicken Feeder

Those of us who raise chickens know that they like to perch on things. This is not generally a problem, but to keep them from roosting on the feed trough and depositing droppings, try this.

First, cut a piece of ½-inch pipe about ⅜ to ½ inch shorter than the span between the ends of the feed trough. Next, drill a small pilot hole in the center of each of two end caps. Glue the end caps onto the pipe. Insert a screw into each hole, leaving ½ inch or so protruding. Set the heads of the screw through the slot or hole in the ends of the trough.

If the trough is made of wood, you can also try this. In each end of the trough, bore a hole to snugly accommodate a short piece of ½-inch PVC pipe. Cut a piece of ¾-inch PVC pipe just slightly shorter than the space between the ends of the trough. Tap one of the ½-inch pieces into place with the ¾-inch piece held in place by it. Tap the other ½-inch piece in place; the two should support the long ¾-inch piece, yet allow it to rotate freely. When a bird tries to perch on the pipe, it will simply roll and keep the bird from getting a good purchase. They will soon quit trying.

Electric-Fence Insulator

Pieces of PVC pipe can be used to make insulators for your electric fence. Take a piece of ¾-inch pipe about 3 to 4 inches long. Cut a slot into the piece's midpoint about ¼ inch deep. Cut angled ends, and drill a hole in each end about ½ inch from the end.

Use the small holes at each end to nail the insulator to the post. Put the fence wire itself into the midpoint slot. Slip a piece of wire 3 or 4 inches long into the insulator, being sure to place it in front of the wire in the slot; bend the wire down at the top and up at the bottom to hold everything in place.

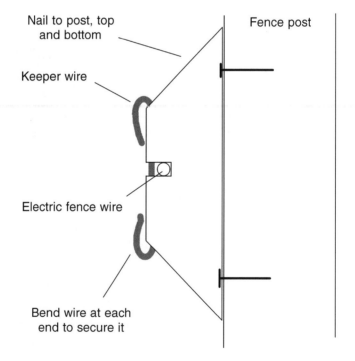

The PVC electric-fence insulator.

Rodent Bait Station 1

Those of us with livestock soon become host to assorted barnyard rodents as well. These animals can eat feed, soil feed, spread disease, and generally be nasty to have around. Sometimes poison baits must be placed to help reduce these vermin. At the same time, any poisons must be kept from pets, livestock, and children. To help in this task, make a safe bait station from 4-inch pipe, a T, and a clean-out.

Cut three pieces of the pipe about 2 feet long. Glue each piece into the T. On the vertical leg of the T, attach the clean-out.

With a piece of furnace duct strap, secure the bait station to a wall where the target animals frequent—usually a spot in the back of the barn, near the feed room. Fill the bait station by way of the clean-out. The target vermin will enter through the arms of the T on the floor and leave with their poisoned booty. Pets, livestock, and children will not be able to see or reach the bait.

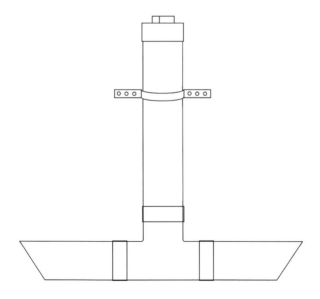

This rodent bait station is useful in barns and sheds where children, livestock, or pets might gain access. It has a threaded plug for filling and two entries for the target animals; it is attached to the wall or post using a metal duct strap.

Rodent Bait Station 2

Another rodent bait station can be made from 4-inch PVC pipe. This one is even simpler, but requires moving it a bit to fill it.

All you need is two pieces of 4-inch pipe about 2 feet long, plus a 90-degree elbow. Glue the pieces together and place the station in a dark corner of the barn after adding a good dose of bait. Again, the rodents will be able to enter and find the bait, but pets, livestock, and children will not be able to see or reach it.

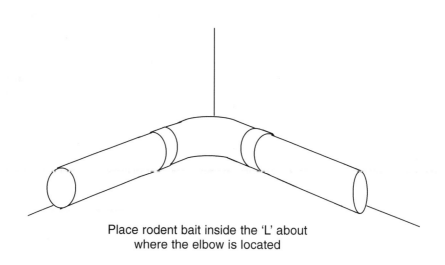

Place rodent bait inside the 'L' about
where the elbow is located

This alternative rodent bait station is even simpler.

Animal Catcher

Sometimes it's just plain difficult to catch an ornery calf or other farmyard critter. To help, here is a simple catcher that nearly anyone can make and use.

You will need an 8- or full 10-foot piece of ¾-inch PVC pipe. Using stout yet flexible nylon line at least ⅜ inch in diameter, make a good slip loop and tightly secure it over one end of the pipe. Run the other end of the rope through the pipe and out the other end. Tie a large knot in the end of the rope or add a chunk of wood (or something similar) to keep the line from being pulled through the pipe.

Use the pipe to extend your reach as you slip the loop over the heads of shy critters you need to catch.

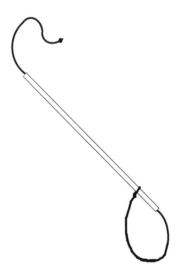

An animal catcher can be made by using a section of ¾-inch PVC pipe and a stout line or rope. Rig it as shown to help catch flighty livestock.

Spike Protector

I use a hay bale spike on the back of my tractor to move the large round bales that I feed our cattle. When not in use, I keep the points of the spike covered with PVC pipe. I used a piece of 3-inch pipe about 2 feet long and glued an end cap on it. This is placed over the large bale spike itself. Over the two smaller spikes, I place pieces of 1½-inch pipe. In the photograph, you can see that I used pieces of PVC pipe extending past the pointed ends of the spikes. If you do this, you will not need to use end caps. This simple project will protect you, along with your kids and any of their friends who might be climbing and playing in the barn.

Bale spike covers.

ATV Toolbox

You can use a piece of 4-, 6-, or 8-inch PVC pipe to make a handy toolbox for your ATV. Place an end cap on one end, and a collar and threaded plug on the other. Attach to your vehicle with large pipe clamps or heavy cable ties. You can keep a tow strap, wrenches, spark plug, and other items inside.

Mower Knife Holder

Most of us who still use sickle-bar mowers for clipping the pastures keep an extra knife or two handy. They have a lot of sharp edges that you can keep covered and protected by attaching a section of 4- or 6-inch PVC pipe to a wall in your shop or implement shed. Simply slide the knives into the pipe to keep them safely covered. A 4-inch-diameter piece of pipe fits snugly around my extra knife. A 6-inch piece would be roomier, but not necessary. Check the fit on your own mower knife by using a scrap of either diameter of pipe.

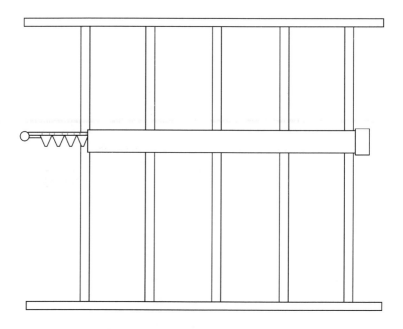

The sharp blade from a sickle-bar mower can be kept safely stored in a section of 6-inch PVC pipe. Mount it on the wall studs of the toolshed and it will be protected and out of the way.

Cellar Vent

If you are fortunate enough to have a root cellar or storm cellar, you can fashion a simple ventilator for it by using PVC pipe. Ventilation is essential to keeping stored produce from rotting by helping to maintain a proper moisture level, along with a good flow of air.

A useful ventilator is seen in the accompanying photograph. It is made from ordinary 4-inch PVC sewer pipe, a T, and two elbows. You may want to wedge a piece of screen wire into the open ends of the pipes to keep wasps and other unwanted critters from gaining access to the pipe.

A good ventilator for a root cellar can be made from PVC pipe.

Three-Point Hitch Carrier Tool Holder

On my three-point hitch carrier, I often have occasion to carry a shovel, ax, or other hand tool. I added this handy holder to help keep any long-handled tool in place and out of the rocks, wood, or other material I'm hauling. It is simply a piece of 4-inch pipe cut to a handy length and bolted to the side of the carrier in a couple of places.

The tool holder on a three-point hitch carrier.

Water Intake Float

Many pond owners use their water source for watering livestock or even domestic tasks. To help keep the water flow free of debris, you can support the water intake by making a simple watertight capsule from a scrap of 4- or 6-inch PVC pipe and a couple of end caps.

Simply use a piece of pipe about 18 to 24 inches long and glue end caps in place. Tie a length of line or wire to the capsule and to the water line near the intake, and allow the float to keep the intake up off the bottom of the pond.

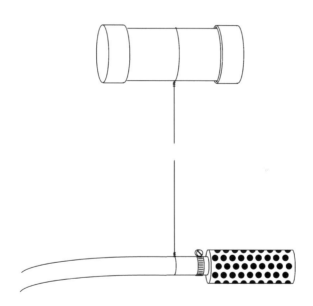

A water intake float made from a scrap of PVC pipe and two end caps.

Water Valve Wrench

A good water valve wrench can be made from a single piece of PVC pipe, a length of threaded rod, and a couple of nuts. This type of wrench is most commonly used on the main water supply valve on your property if you have a rural or municipal water system. The valve is usually located inside a riser and is not always easy to reach to shut off if you need to make a repair to your water system.

First, determine the size and type of water shutoff valve that you have. Next, take a piece of 1½- or 2-inch PVC pipe in a length that will make it convenient to use. I'd make it so that when it is in place on the valve, the upper end is at about waist height. In the end of the pipe, cut a slot just wide enough to slip over the water valve shutoff.

In the upper end of the pipe, drill two holes that are directly in line with the slot. Slide the threaded rod through the holes and put a nut on each side. Tighten the nuts snugly. That's it; the wrench is ready to use. By making it so that the handle lines up with the slot, it is easier to put the wrench in place on the valve shutoff.

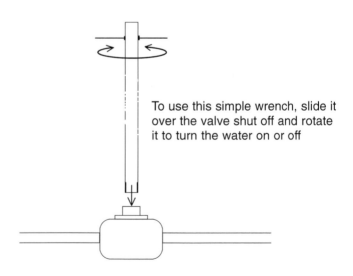

To use this simple wrench, slide it over the valve shut off and rotate it to turn the water on or off

A water valve shutoff wrench made from PVC pipe.

Sign Frame

A simple sign frame can be made from three pieces of pipe and two elbows. Simply plan it for the sign you have. Cut the legs long enough to be tapped into the ground. Hang the sign from the crosspiece, and you're in business.

This sign frame uses whatever materials you have on hand.

5

IN THE WORKSHOP

Tool Holder 2

I have a spot in my garage where I need to keep a screwdriver handy. To do that, I simply cut a piece of ¾-inch PVC pipe about 10 inches long. I drilled holes in it to accommodate a couple of screws and attached it to a post in the garage. I simply drop the screwdriver into the pipe, and it's there when I need it.

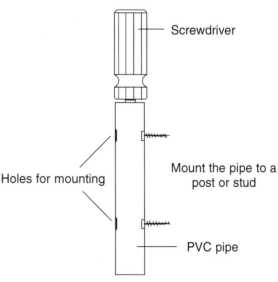

This simple holder keeps a screwdriver handy for special jobs.

Hammer Carrier

Cut a piece of 1½-inch PVC pipe about 3 to 3½ inches long. Cut two vertical slots about ¼ inch wide, 2½ inches deep, and 1 inch apart on one side of the pipe. Thread these slots down over your belt; you can slip your hammer into the pipe while you work on a project.

A PVC hammer holder keeps projects easy.

A Note About Plumbing Your
Workshop for Compressed Air

I have heard of folks using CPVC pipe to plumb in air compressor fittings around their garage or workshop. CPVC pipe is manufactured to withstand about 120 pounds per square inch (psi) of pressure. This is normally sufficient to handle the air pressure generated by the standard garage and workshop air compressor.

However, manufacturers do not recommend the use of CPVC pipe for plumbing of air compressor systems. They note that shattering and flying shards of pipe can result if the pipe fails. With that in mind, I must state that I can't and don't advocate bypassing manufacturer recommendations for using CPVC pipe for this purpose. I do not have my air compressor plumbed with CPVC pipe, nor do I plan to do so.

Extension Cord Tamer

Handy holders to keep light extension cords coiled and out of the way can be made easily by cutting 1½-inch PVC pipe into 1- to 1½-inch sections. Smooth the cut edges with a bit of sandpaper. Slip a ring over a coiled cord and it will stay nicely coiled.

Welding Rod Belt Carrier

When doing a welding job, it's often handy to have an extra supply of rods available quickly. Here is a quick and easy way to make a carrier for welding rods that threads right onto your belt. You'll have extra rods readily available.

Simply take a piece of 2- or 3-inch PVC pipe about 12 to 13 inches long. Most rods are 14 inches long, and you'll want an inch or so protruding from the top. About 1½ inches from one end of the pipe, drill a pilot hole that will let you insert a narrow saber saw blade. Repeat this where you see the X's in the drawing. Cut the slots with your saber saw, making them wide and long enough to let you thread your belt through them.

Glue a plain end cap onto the bottom and you are ready to go.

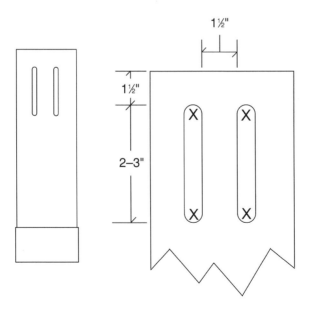

A welding rod carrier for your belt.

Welding Rod Storage

Welding rods should be kept in a dry environment. To help keep them dry, you can make this simple container from PVC pipe and a couple of fittings.

First, cut a piece of 3- or 4-inch PVC pipe about 14½ to 15 inches long. Welding rods are generally 14 inches long, so this will allow plenty of room. Glue an end cap on one end. On the other end, glue a threaded collar. All that is left to do is to put in the welding rods and close the container with the threaded plug.

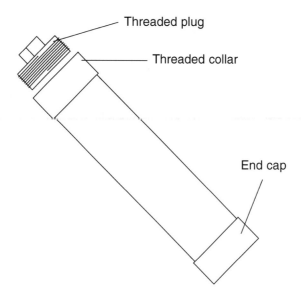

Threaded plug

Threaded collar

End cap

The welding rod storage container.

Sanding Shaper

Take a scrap piece of 1½- or 2-inch PVC and wrap a piece of sand-paper around it. This makes it easier to shape and smooth curves.

Grease-Gun Holder

To make a handy holder for your grease gun, cut a piece of 3-inch PVC pipe about 14 inches long and bolt it to a handy spot on your tractor fender, combine sheet metal, or in your shop or garage. It will keep your grease gun handy and available. Just drop the gun down into the pipe, hooking the lever handle over the side. The 14-inch length should completely cover the body of the gun.

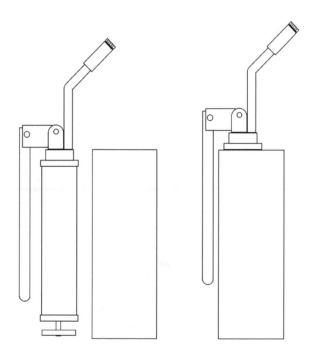

A PVC holder keeps your grease gun ready for use.

Shovel Holder

A similar holder for a shovel or manure fork can be made from a length of 3- or 4-inch PVC pipe. Make it long enough to cover the handle, if possible, and bolt it at an angle onto the front or side of your utility trailer or manure spreader. Placing it at an angle will keep it from bouncing out.

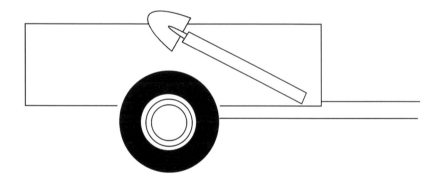

A piece of 2-inch PVC pipe bolted onto the side of your utility trailer can help keep your shovel handy.

Shop Vacuum Extension

If you have hard-to-reach nooks and crannies in your home or shop, try this. Locate a size of PVC pipe that will attach to your particular make of vacuum and attach it to the end of the hose. You may need to use a hacksaw to split the end of the pipe just a bit to get it to fit down over the vacuum hose end. You can also use a hacksaw to cut an angled end on the new vac attachment, or heat it gently and compress the end to get a narrow tip.

Here at home, we use a length of ¾-inch PVC pipe attached to our household vacuum cleaner tube to suck up the many ladybugs that plague us each fall. They love the light-colored cathedral ceilings in the house. We merely used some duct tape to attach the pipe to one of the vacuum extension tubes. It helps us reach the 13-foot peak in the ceiling.

Tool Handle Soaker

In my book *The Self-Reliant Homestead—A Book of Country Skills* (Burford Books, 2003), I describe how linseed oil is used to preserve the wooden handles of tools. There, I advise using an old jersey glove to apply the oil. Here is another, neater idea. Take a length of 1½- or 3-inch PVC pipe just a bit longer than the longest tool handle you will be working with. Glue an end cap on one end. Secure the pipe in a vertical position to a solid support and drop the tool, handle-first, into the tube. Then you can just pour in a quantity of linseed oil and let the handle soak up all the preservative it can. When you are finished with your tools, merely pour the oil back into the original container.

Make a shorter soaker using 1½- or 2-inch pipe to use for hammers, hatchets, and other tools with short handles.

Parts Tray

A simple parts tray can be made by using PVC pipe. First, mark and—using a band saw or table saw—split an appropriate length of 4-inch pipe into halves.

Trace along the inside of the pipe onto a piece of scrap lumber and cut out a half-moon-shaped piece for each end. Drill a few small holes around the ends of the pipe and secure the wood ends using small nails. You can repeat this process to put tray dividers at points in the tray.

You can also use a PVC end cap for the ends of the tray. It must be accurately marked before it is cut into two pieces. Then it is simply attached to the split pipe using PVC cement. Stabilize the tray by attaching the ends (whether wood or PVC) to short pieces of 1 × 4 or similar-sized wood.

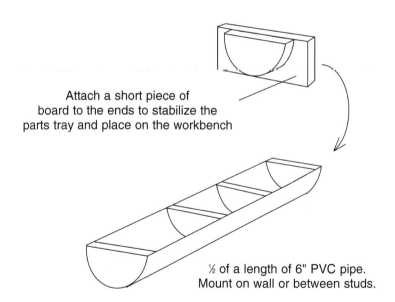

Attach a short piece of
board to the ends to stabilize the
parts tray and place on the workbench

½ of a length of 6" PVC pipe.
Mount on wall or between studs.

PVC pipe makes a nifty parts tray.

Garage Utility Hanger

Need a hanger or two in your garage where you can hang a bicycle, garden hose, or other items? You can easily make one from some scraps of 1½-inch PVC pipe and four elbows. Make it to fit the joists in your garage as well as the item to be suspended.

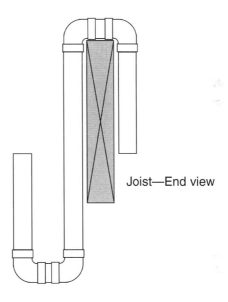

Joist—End view

A handy hanger for your garage or workshop is easily made from PVC pipe.

Dowel and Short-Stock Storage

I am a saver. I save scraps of lumber, pieces of sheet metal, and just about anything else that I think I might have a use for later.

If you are the same, here is an idea to help you store short lengths of molding, dowel rods, and any other small, short stock.

Begin with a sturdy wooden box. Cut pieces of scrap 4-inch PVC pipe into lengths to accommodate the items you plan to store and organize. I recommend cutting some just a bit taller than the sides of the box, some about a foot longer than that, still more another foot taller . . . you get the idea. Line these up in rows in your box and begin "filing" your short scraps of dowel rods, moldings, light wood, and other items. Consider adding some casters to allow you to move the storage container around your workshop.

As an alternative, consider using a heavy plastic tub as a main container. The wheels can be added by attaching them to a plywood base and securing the tub to it.

Small-Item Holder

A smaller version of the dowel and small-stock holder can be made to fit right on your worktable or bench. Make these individually by gluing an end cap on a piece of 3- or 4-inch pipe as shown. You can also make a larger holder by using a small wooden box, plastic tub, or container, adding appropriately sized lengths of 1½- to 3-inch sections of PVC pipe. This handy holder can be used to keep pencils, artist's brushes, small files, small brushes, and countless other items neat and available on the workbench.

This benchtop holder is made from a short piece of PVC pipe and an end cap.

Handy Hanger for Your Ladder

If your extension ladder is one that has hollow rungs, try this hanger. Take a short scrap of ½- or ¾-inch PVC pipe and insert it through a rung of your extension ladder to give you a place to hang your paint can. With a hacksaw or rasp, cut a notch in the pipe to keep the paint can bail from slipping. Once inserted, you can wedge the pipe in with a small piece of wood to help keep it in place. I made a small wire clip to keep the bail from accidentally getting bumped from the notch and off the hanger.

This hanger keeps the paint can within easy reach.

Handsaw Protector

To protect the cutting edge of your favorite handsaw, cut a piece of
½-inch PVC pipe to the same length as the saw blade. With your
table saw, *carefully* make a split completely down one side of the
pipe. Put the split pipe over the saw edge. If the cut is too wide to
hold snugly in place by itself, secure it with a couple of rubber bands
cut from old auto or bicycle inner tubes.

Glue-Gun Holder

If you use a cordless drill or even a hot-glue gun a lot at your work-bench, you will like this handy holster to keep your tool out or the way, but in reach.

Take a 45-degree 4-inch PVC elbow. Drill a couple of ¼- to ⅜-inch holes in on one side of the piece. Drill two more smaller holes 180 degrees around the coupler. These holes will allow you to attach the holder to the workbench leg or side. The larger holes will accommodate a screwdriver; the smaller holes will hold screws.

Position the elbow so that it will hold your drill or glue gun without it tipping out. You may need to use a hacksaw to cut a notch to keep the gun or drill trigger from being depressed.

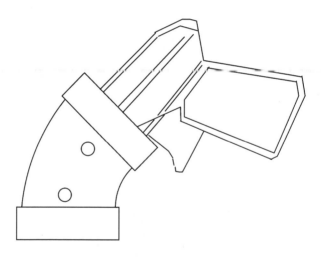

Keep tools out of the way but still handy with this holder.

Bungee Storage

A length of PVC pipe can come in handy as bungee cord storage. Begin with a piece of 4-inch pipe. You can use a large 1- to 1½-inch drill bit to cut a few holes at points to accommodate different lengths of bungee cords. Attach the holder to the wall with heavy screws.

Oil-Can Holder

I've got one of the old trigger-type oil cans that's always on my workbench. Unfortunately, it often got tipped over, and I'd come in to the shop to find oil all over the bench. I've solved the problem by using a piece of 3-inch PVC pipe about 3 inches long. I glued an end cap in place and screwed the assembly to the workbench top. The oil can is set into the plastic tube, keeping it upright.

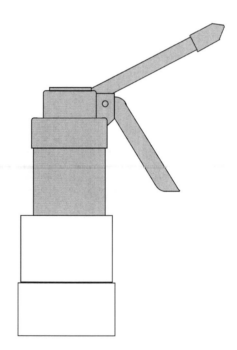

*This oil-can holder will prevent spills and can be
attached directly to the workbench.*

Spool Tamer

This idea is supersimple but superhandy.

I purchase weed trimmer line in large spools. It used to be difficult to keep the line from going wild when I tried to pull off a length to load onto my trimmer. I solved the problem in this way.

Bore a hole into a flat surface—a corner of the workbench or the like—that will snugly accommodate a piece of ½-inch PVC pipe. Tap the pipe into place. Slip the spool of trimmer line down over the pipe. It is now easy to pull the correct length of line off the spool without it going everywhere.

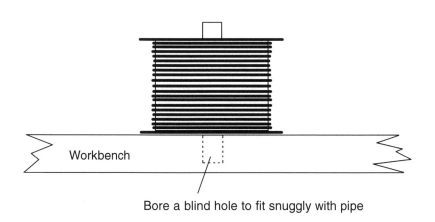

Workbench

Bore a blind hole to fit snuggly with pipe

Keep your weed trimmer line handy with this simple spool tamer.

Spring Clamps

Some simple spring clamps for the home workshop can be made by cutting lengths of 1½-, 3-, or 4-inch pieces of PVC pipe into rings ½ inch to 1½ inches long. Split one side of each of the rings. Spread the ends and place them over project pieces to hold them together when gluing or nailing.

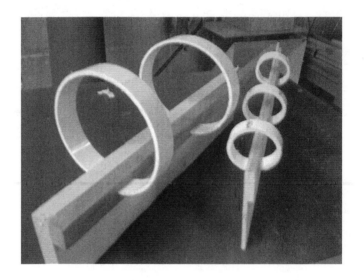

PVC makes a simple and inexpensive clamp.

File Storage

To keep files like new, slip a piece of PVC with a cap over them. Write the size and type of file on the pipe with a permanent marker, and you won't have to always hunt for the right one in the bottom of the toolbox or on the workbench.

Level Case

I keep my string level in a handy little case made from PVC pipe. I simply cut a piece of ½-inch pipe just a bit longer than the level—about 3 inches or so. Then I glued an end cap on one end. On the other end, I slip an end cap on and off as I need to. I painted the small case bright orange to help me keep from misplacing it.

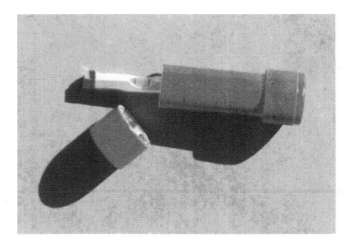

This small case protects a string level.

6

MISCELLANEOUS PROJECTS

Map Case

A tough and durable map case can be made from a piece of 3- or 4-inch PVC pipe. Simply cut a piece long enough to hold your maps. Add an end cap on one end and a threaded cap and collar on the other.

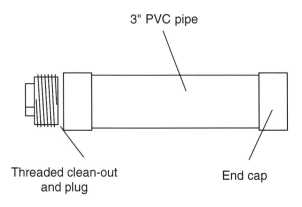

3" PVC pipe

Threaded clean-out
and plug

End cap

Protect your maps in PVC cases.

Target Stand 1

For plinking and target shooting around the place, you need a good target stand. Here is a simple one to make from scrap PVC pipe and a few fittings. Use some stout wire to make a couple of S-hooks; hang the target backing from those. Build it large or small enough to suit your needs. Note that PVC pipe does not hold up well to being shot. Concentrate on your marksmanship when using these stands!

A simple target stand made from a few fittings and some short pieces of pipe.

Target Stand 2

Another durable target stand can be made from two pieces of 1-inch PVC pipe about 2½ to 3 feet long. Simply take each piece and cut one end at a shallow angle to enable it to be driven into the ground. Next, set your table saw for a shallow cut, and make a slot in each piece from the square end, a foot or so down the length of the piece.

To use this simple target stand, take a piece of ordinary corrugated cardboard of a convenient width. Tap the slotted pipes into the ground that width apart, with the slots facing each other. Then just slide the cardboard into the slots and staple up your target.

Use a pair of these slotted pipes to support a cardboard target.

Target Stand 3

Yet another simple target holder can be made by cutting a slot about 3 or 4 inches deep in the end of a piece of PVC pipe. Drive or push the holder into the ground and slide the target into the slot.

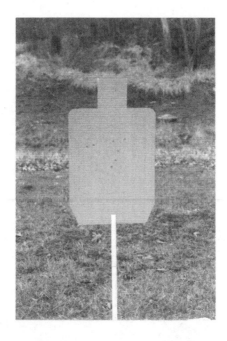

A simple target stand can be made by cutting a slot in the end of a piece of PVC pipe.

Time Capsule

Here is a fun project for the whole family. You can preserve loads of interesting memorabilia and information about your family and era for your descendants to enjoy and learn from.

To begin, locate a piece of PVC pipe in as large a diameter as you can find. Eight- to 12-inch-diameter pipe will be best, if you can get it. Next, glue an end cap on one end. On the other end, decide if you want to use a threaded collar and plug, or simply glue on another end cap once the time capsule is filled.

Here are some ideas of things to include in your family time capsule:

• A CD of your backed-up computer hard drive.

• Family photographs (printed onto acid-free paper for long life). Consider including photos of each family member taken over a period of time—as a baby, growing up, as a young adult, and so on. Write labels on the backs in indelible ink.

• Favorite family recipes.

• Coins and postage stamps—maybe a few old ones, along with the current year's coins or stamps. Some of your state quarters would make a nifty addition, as would any of the interesting stamps currently available.

• Journals. These can include all kinds of information, observations, and thoughts.

• A CD of your favorite music.

• A DVD of a favorite movie.

• A local newspaper. These provide all kinds of information of the day.

• Write a letter to include in the capsule. Describe what life is like where you live now. Include neat traditions and things about your family.

• Think of other items unique to your family that you want to include.

Probably the oldest method of preserving your time capsule is to bury it. You can also construct a simple form and cast it into a special decorative "cornerstone" that can be placed near your front steps, in your flower garden, or wherever you choose. Or just put the capsule into a safe or vault.

It's also a good idea to take a picture of the capsule and/or location where you have placed it and slip this into an envelope. Place the envelope in a safe-deposit box, behind a picture frame, or in another place where you or your descendants can find it.

Rhythm Sticks

Kids enjoy these simple toys, and they are easy to make. It's a fun project you can do together.

Cut two pieces of ½- or ¾-inch PVC pipe 12 to 16 inches long. Lightly sand the pipe to remove any printing. Drill a small hole in each of four end caps. Through the holes, thread some string or ribbon; knot each string heavily on the inside of the cap so it won't pull out. Attach a few beads or feathers to the outside ends of the ribbons or strings. Glue one end cap to each of the pipes. Add a dozen or so BBs or kernels of popcorn to each pipe. Glue on the other end cap after testing the shaker to be sure you like its rattle. Add some colored tape or paint the pipe tubes. You can even sprinkle glitter into the paint before it dries.

Fishing Rod Holders

Everyone needs to find some fishing time. Here is a way to keep your fishing rod in place while you kick back.

Cut a piece of 1½-inch PVC pipe about 12 to 16 inches long. With your band saw or saber saw, cut a slanted tip on one end. This will go into the ground. On the other, glue a 45-degree elbow. Into that, glue another piece of 1½-inch pipe about 3 inches long. To that piece, line up and glue a 1½-inch T.

To use the rod holder, just shove the pointed end of the pipe into the soil. Slip the rod handle into the elevated side of the T, and you're in business.

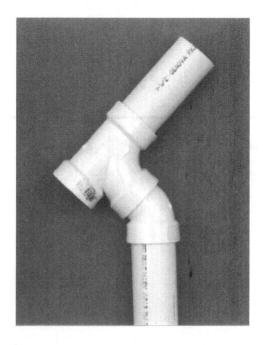

Relax while you fish with this PVC rod holder.

Wind Chimes

You know, there is something special about sitting out on the front porch, sipping a cup of tea, and enjoying a cool evening. That relaxed feeling is complemented by the addition of simple yet melodious wind chimes. The gentle melodies of wind chimes do indeed entertain and relax. The slightest breeze artfully plays a tune upon this simple instrument.

The chimes described here have a sort of wooden or bamboo tone to them. In making these PVC wind chimes, I used ¾-inch pipe. To determine the length and suspension points for each of the tubes, I referred to the chart in my earlier book *The Self-Reliant Homestead*. After cutting the tubes to the correct length, I carefully drilled the holes for each suspension clip.

Just what is the proper length for the tubes? Good question. And in doing some research on this, I learned that just as important as the length of the tube is the point at which the tube is suspended. Having studied radio and radio waves some, and being a student of the guitar, I realized that there are points on a sound wave, much like a radio wave, where the tone sounds "alive," and other points where it is a "dead" tone. Below are the dimensions for making a set of chimes using ¾-inch pipe.

NOTE	LENGTH (IN INCHES)	SUSPENSION POINT (IN INCHES)
F	17⅞	4
G flat	17⅜	3⅞
G	16⅞	3¾
A flat	16⅜	3¹¹⁄₁₆
A	15¹⁵⁄₁₆	3⁹⁄₁₆
B flat	15⁷⁄₁₆	3⁷⁄₁₆

Take a look at the illustration to see how to use a short piece of stiff wire to suspend each tube. Heavy fishing line makes a good support. Suspend the musical tubes from a rounded and smoothed wooden disc.

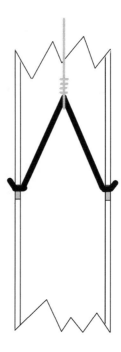

Use a V-shaped wire to suspend each tube.

The diameter of the clapper and the size of the paddle-like wind catcher will help determine just how much—or little—wind it will take to make your chimes . . . chime. If you want to hear music with the slightest breeze, then a larger clapper with very little clearance between it and the tubes will make music with just a wisp of wind. If you don't like the chimes to keep you awake all night, then consider a smaller clapper that takes more movement to strike the tubes. Similarly, a large wind catcher at the bottom of the set will get the tubes ringing more easily than a smaller one.

Fishing Limbline

More and more river fishermen are using limblines made from ¾-inch PVC pipe. These springy poles are handy to make, simple to use, and easy to locate. Some anglers who run their lines at night add reflector tape to make them even easier to spot. Here in Indiana, you can fish up to 10 of them as long as they are marked with your name and address.

Many fishermen tie the line securely down toward the base of the pole and wrap it around as they go toward the tip. Tie it off again at the tip and the let it dangle into the water with the baited hook attached. The extra line adds a measure of security just in case the pipe gets broken or the top loop slips off.

When using this device, be sure to check your local regulations first.

Antenna Insulator

I'm a radio buff. I have used PVC to help erect antennas for pulling in distant radio stations. PVC pipe can also be used to make insulators for wire antennas. Simply take a 3- to 6-inch piece of ½-inch PVC pipe and drill holes completely through it on both ends. The antenna wire will be attached to one end, the support wire to the other. The pipe will prevent the antenna wire from grounding to the support line.

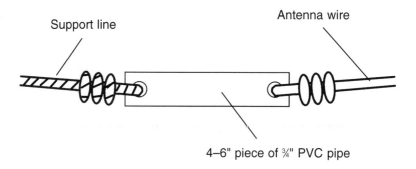

PVC pipe can keep antennas safe.

Handy Boat Paddle

If you need a boat paddle to stow in case of an emergency, try this. The paddle likely will not withstand constant use, but it will certainly suffice if your motor conks out or if you run out of gas while afloat.

First, lay out the blade design on a piece of ⅜- or ½-inch plywood. It should be about 18 to 20 inches long. Mark it so that it is about 6 to 8 inches wide at the bottom and for about two-thirds of its length. At that point, taper it to about 4 inches wide at the top. Cut out the blade, smooth the edges, and seal with polyurethane varnish.

For the handle, use 1½-inch PVC pipe in a length that comes up to about your chest. Cut a slot in one end of the pipe the same width as the thickness of the plywood blade and about 8 to 12 inches long. Slip the plywood blade into place. You may want to rip an 8- to 12-inch piece of wooden closet rod and insert the resulting half-moon-shaped pieces into the cavity between the blade and plastic pipe to increase the sturdiness. Drill two or three holes up and down the handle through the paddle blade and secure it with bolts, washers, and nuts. You can put and end cap on the upper end of the pipe, or attach a T to help you get a grip on it.

This handy boat paddle is easy to make and keep aboard your boat for an emergency.

Controlling Nuisance Beavers

If your place is located adjacent to beaver habitat, then you have likely experienced the frustrations of seeing the flat-tailed wood chompers enlarge their domain and inundate a part of your property. Besides humans, beavers may be the only animals that actually manipulate their habitat to suit their needs. Often, though, those changes are incompatible with our own plans for the same chunk of real estate. Simply tearing out a beaver dam is rarely effective. The critters will build it back or repair it overnight.

Probably the most effective device to control water levels in a beaver pond is a something called the Clemson beaver pond leveler. Developed at Clemson University, it has proven effective in allowing continual water flow and facilitating the manipulation of water levels in beaver ponds for moist-soil management that is beneficial for migratory waterfowl and shorebirds.

The Clemson beaver pond leveler consists of a 10-inch-diameter perforated PVC pipe encased in heavy-gauge galvanized hog wire. The encased portion is placed upstream of the dam or blocked culvert in the deepest part of the stream. It is connected to nonperforated sections of PVC pipe that are run through the dam or culvert to a water control structure downstream.

To manipulate the water level of the pond, attach an elbow to the downstream end with a pipe extending up to the desired water level. The Clemson beaver pond leveler works best in relatively flat locations. It is effective because beavers cannot detect the sound of falling or flowing water as the pond or culvert drains. Therefore, they do not try to plug the pipe.

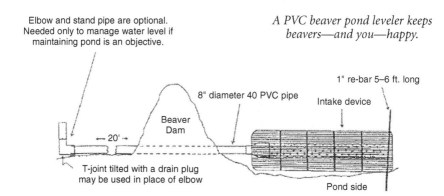

Elbow and stand pipe are optional. Needed only to manage water level if maintaining pond is an objective.

A PVC beaver pond leveler keeps beavers—and you—happy.

1" re-bar 5–6 ft. long

8" diameter 40 PVC pipe

Intake device

Beaver Dam

← 20' →

T-joint tilted with a drain plug may be used in place of elbow

Pond side

7

MAKING FURNITURE FROM PVC PIPE

PVC pipe has become popular enough for furniture making that manufacturers now offer special fittings just to make the furniture maker's job easier. These fittings also result in a more streamlined and functional piece of furniture. Entire books have been written just on the subject of PVC furniture making.

For the average workshop warrior, I'm including a couple of plans that will turn out nice PVC furniture. These plans call for ordinary plumbing fittings and pipe and no specialized fittings.

At the end of the section, several sources of furniture-specific hardware and some texts for further reading are listed.

Chair

Here is a simple design for a durable chair to place on your patio or porch.

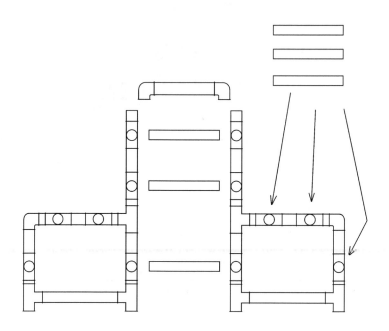

An easy, durable outdoor chair made from PVC.

Table/Cart (using lawn mower wheels)

Using some T's, elbows, and 2-inch pipe, you can make a nice little table or cart for your patio, deck, or workshop.

As shown in the drawing, make up two of the cart halves. Each half will require six T's, two elbows, and two end caps. Join them together with lengths of pipe as wide as you want the table or cart to be. Remember that the fittings will add some width to the finished assembly.

If you want, attach a couple of lawn mower wheels by first drilling holes about ½ inch above the end caps at the end of the legs on one end. You will probably need to use some washers between the pipe and the wheel. Two or three should be plenty. They will serve as spacers to prevent the wheels from rubbing the pipe.

For the tabletop, you can use plywood or boards. If you are using plywood, just attach it with a bolt in each corner. You can attach boards with one or two bolts on each end, depending upon the width of the board.

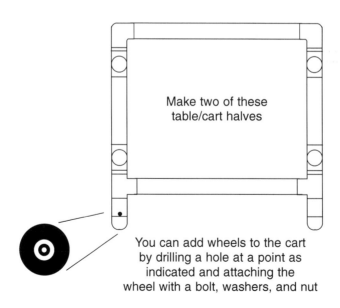

Make two of these
table/cart halves

You can add wheels to the cart
by drilling a hole at a point as
indicated and attaching the
wheel with a bolt, washers, and nut

This piece is made from PVC, fittings, and boards.

PVC FURNITURE SOURCES

For furniture parts, fittings, and plans try these sources:

C&S Plastics, Inc.
1550 5th Street SW
Winter Haven, FL 33880
1-800-476-0823

Savko Plastic Pipe & Fittings, Inc.
683 East Lincoln Avenue
Columbus, OH 43229
1-877-885-4445
www.savko.com

A to Z Supply
13396 Ridge Road
Grass Valley, CA 95945
530-273-6608
www.atozsupply.com

FURTHER READING ON PVC FURNITURE

- *PVC Furniture* (Weekend Workshop Collection) by Edward A. Baldwin

- *PVC Furniture: 27 Easy-to-Build, Inexpensive, Last Forever Projects* from Workman Publishers

- *How to Make PVC Pipe Furniture: For Indoors & Outdoors* by Ed and Steve Baldwin

- For a great Web site pertaining to PVC furniture, check out www.pvcplans.com. It offer loads of information.

INDEX